Hairy Harry

Belle Perez

These are grass seeds.

Grass seeds grow into grass.

What makes seeds grow into plants?
Make a Hairy Harry and find out!
You will need:

Cut the stocking.

Put grass seeds in the toe of the stocking.

Put soil in the stocking.

Make the soil into a head shape.

Tie the end of the stocking.

Put the stocking in a jar of water.

Keep adding water to keep the stocking wet.

After two weeks, the grass will start to grow.

Look at Hairy Harry now!